DATE DUE			

NEW ZEALAND

Geoff Burns

General Editor

Henry Pluckrose

Franklin Watts

London New York Sydney Toronto

Facts About New Zealand

Area:
The three main islands total 267,000 sq. km. (103,000 sq. miles). This is about the same size as Britain or Japan

Population:
3,158,200 (1982)

Capital:
Wellington

Largest cities:
Auckland, Wellington, Hamilton, Christchurch, Dunedin

Official language:
English. Some Maoris use their own language

Main religion:
Christianity

Major exports:
Meat, dairy products, wool, fruit, fish, forestry products

Currency:
Dollars

Franklin Watts Limited
12a Golden Square
London W1

ISBN: UK Edition 0 86313 061 5
ISBN: US Edition 0 531 03761-4
Library of Congress Catalog Card No:
83-50111

© Franklin Watts Limited 1983

Typeset by Ace Filmsetting Ltd,
Frome, Somerset
Printed in Hong Kong

Text Editor: Brenda Williams
Maps: Tony Payne
Design: Peter Benoist
Photographs: All Sport, 26; G. D. Burns,
17, 21, 27; I. B. Burns, 10, 18, 28; L. S.
Burns, 3, 5, 6; Chris Fairclough, 7, 11,
13, 15, 20, 23; J. P. Hollinrake, 22, 29,
31; P. M. Muller, 4, 30; New Zealand
High Commission, London, 12, 14, 16,
19, 24, 25
Front Cover: Mount Cook (Zefa)
Back Cover: Zefa

In 1769 Captain James Cook became the first European to sail round the two main islands that make up New Zealand. He landed on the North Island, near the spot where his statue now stands.

The South Island has a large
mountain range called the Southern
Alps. It runs the length of the long,
narrow island. Mount Cook lies at
the heart of the Southern Alps and
reaches 3,763 m (12,349 feet) at its
peak. It is the highest mountain in
New Zealand.

Some areas of New Zealand are still in their wild state. Many national parks have been set up to protect this land for people to enjoy. Wild areas are called the bush. Some of the plants which grow there are found nowhere else in the world.

New Zealand has long stretches of beautiful coastline. Most of its people live in cities near the sea. No part of the country is more than 112 km (70 miles) from the coast.

New Zealanders love outdoor sports and competitions. In the hot summer months they enjoy yachting, as well as swimming and surfing, especially in the north of the North Island.

This picture shows some stamps and money used in New Zealand. The main unit of currency is the dollar, which is divided into 100 cents.

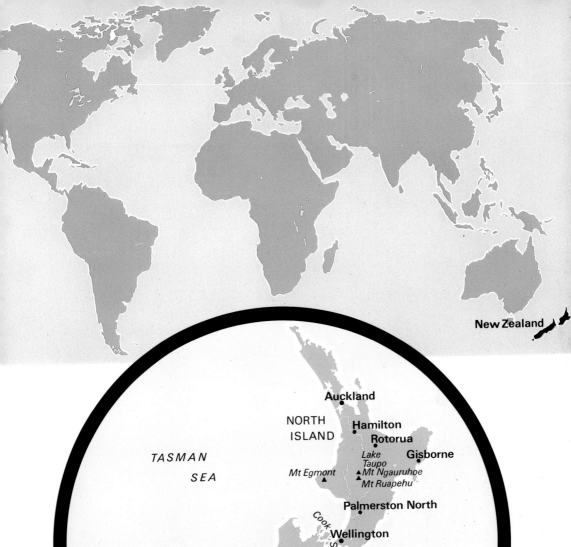

New Zealand

NORTH ISLAND

TASMAN SEA

- Auckland
- Hamilton
- Rotorua
- Gisborne

Lake Taupo

Mt Egmont ▲ ▲ *Mt Ngauruhoe*
▲ *Mt Ruapehu*

- Palmerston North

Cook Strait

- Wellington

NEW ZEALAND

PACIFIC OCEAN

Alps

Mt Cook ▲

- Christchurch

Southern

Lake Wanaka
Lake
Lake Wakatipu
Te Anau

SOUTH ISLAND

- Dunedin

- Invercargill
- Bluff
Foveaux Strait
Stewart Island

9

Most New Zealanders are descended from British settlers. But one in every ten is part-Maori. Legends tell that the Maoris came from the Pacific Islands over 600 years ago. They arrived in seven great canoes, like the one shown above. Maoris named the country Aotearoa, which means Land of the Long White Cloud.

Maori meeting places are called the Marae. Maoris gather on the Marae for speeches, ceremonies, and other public meetings. Here a group waits outside the traditional meeting house. It is decorated with faces and figures. These show the wood-carving skills for which the Maoris are famous.

Auckland is New Zealand's biggest city. It sprawls across the top of the North Island, stretching from the Pacific Ocean on one side to the Tasman Sea on the other.

New Zealand has 3 million people, and of these over a quarter live in Auckland. Many Maoris and people from the Pacific Islands have made their homes there. The weather is warm all year.

Wellington has been the capital city since 1865. It is set among hills on the southern tip of the North Island. The ferry that crosses the Cook Strait to the South Island leaves from Wellington. It is one of the main ports of New Zealand.

The main government building in Wellington is called the Beehive. It is used by members of the New Zealand parliament. New Zealand is a fully independent, self-governing member of the Commonwealth.

Children between the ages of 6 and 15 must go to school. New Zealand's children spend a lot of their school-time out of doors, both at work and play. Schooling is free.

New Zealand's oldest university is
Otago, part of which can be seen
here. The university is in Dunedin.
Dunedin was settled by pioneers from
Scotland. It was one of the country's
first settlements.

Most families in New Zealand own their homes. The houses are mainly made of wood, but many in the South Island are built of bricks or concrete blocks. Looking after houses and gardens is a popular pastime.

New Zealanders enjoy family life.
They spend much of their spare time
out of doors and near water, perhaps
on the beach or picnicking by a river.

Dairy farming is important, especially in the North Island. Most dairy farms have a herd of about 120 cows and are usually smaller than sheep farms. Mechanized milking was begun in New Zealand, which is one of the world's largest producers of butter and cheese.

Most of the goods that New Zealand sends abroad come from its farms. The country has recently begun to sell forestry products, wine and fruit, as well as traditional meat, wool and dairy products.

For every person in New Zealand there are at least 20 sheep! Many of the flocks are kept on big sheep stations in the hills of the South Island. New Zealand lamb is famous all over the world. The first shipment of frozen lamb left the country in 1882.

Fishermen come from many other countries to join the local boats around New Zealand. They catch many types of fish, such as tuna, squid, snapper and barracuda. Large oyster beds lie in the Foveaux Strait between the tip of the South Island and the smaller Stewart Island.

The kiwi is a bird that cannot fly. It is found only in New Zealand, where it feeds at night in the bush. New Zealanders are often called 'Kiwis' as the bird is one of the country's emblems.

Over half a million tourists visit New Zealand each year. Many come to see the hot thermal springs that gush from the ground near Rotorua in the North Island. The lakes and mountains of the South Island are popular for bus tours.

Rugby football is one of the many games enjoyed in New Zealand. The famous All Blacks take their name from the clothes they wear. On their shirts is another national symbol, the silver fern. The All Black team here is taking part in the Haka, a traditional Maori war-dance which is performed before their games.

New Zealand is proud of its famous personalities, such as athlete John Walker. Others are the opera singer Dame Kiri Te Kanawa, athlete Peter Snell and mountaineer Sir Edmund Hillary.

The North Island has many geysers, hot springs and boiling mud pools. There are also volcanoes, both active and extinct. Mounts Ngauruhoe, Ruapehu and Tongariro are the largest.

Glaciers are rivers of ice. In New Zealand they flow slowly from the Southern Alps toward the sea. The best known are the Fox, the Tasman and the Franz Joseph glaciers.

Most of the country's electricity comes from hydroelectric stations on lakes and rivers. But underground heat is also used to make power. At geothermal stations, hot steam forced from the ground produces electricity. This station is at Wairakei.

Bluff is on the southern tip of the South Island. New Zealand is midway between the Equator and the South Pole, and a long way from any other country. This sign points the way to lands across the sea.

Index

All Blacks 26
Auckland 12–13

Beehive 15
Bluff 31

Captain Cook 3
Commonwealth 15
Cook Strait 14

Dairy farming 20–21
Dunedin 17

Fishing 23
Foveaux Strait 23

Geyser 28
Glacier 29

Kiwi 24

Maori 10–11, 13, 26
Marae 11
Money 8
Mount Cook 4

National parks 5
North Island 3, 7, 25, 28

Otago 17

Pacific Islands 10, 13
Pacific Ocean 12

Rotorua 25

Scotland 17
Sheep farming 20–22
Southern Alps 4, 29
South Island 3, 4, 14, 18,
    22–23, 25, 29, 31
Stamps 8
Stewart Island 23
Surfing 7
Swimming 7

Tasman Sea 12

Volcanoes 28

Wairakei 30
Wellington 14, 15

Yachting 7